Ripley's MIGHTY MACHINES

Believe *It* or Not!®

Ripley PUBLISHING

a Jim Pattison Company

TWISTS

Written by Ian Graham

Consultant Chris Oxlade

PUBLISHING

Publisher Anne Marshall

Managing Editor Rebecca Miles
Picture Researcher James Proud
Editors Lisa Regan, Rosie Alexander
Assistant Editor Amy Harrison
Proofreader Judy Barratt
Indexer Hilary Bird

Art Director Sam South
Design Rocket Design (East Anglia) Ltd
Reprographics Stephan Davis

www.ripleys.com

Copyright ©2009 by Ripley Entertainment Inc.

First published in Great Britain in 2009 by
Random House Books
Random House, 20 Vauxhall Bridge Road,
London SW1V 2SA

www.rbooks.co.uk

Addresses for companies within The Random House
Group Limited can be found at:
www.randomhouse.co.uk/offices.htm

The Random House Group Limited Reg. No. 954009

ISBN 9780099543640

10 9 8 7 6 5 4 3 2 1

The Random House Group Limited supports The Forest
Stewardship Council (FSC), the leading international
forest certification organisation. All our titles that are
printed on Greenpeace approved FSC certified paper
carry the FSC logo. Our paper procurement policy can be
found at www.rbooks.co.uk/environment

A CIP catalogue record for this book
is available from the British Library

Printed in China

PUBLISHER'S NOTE
While every effort has been made to verify the accuracy
of the entries in this book, the Publishers cannot be held
responsible for any errors contained in the work. They
would be glad to receive any information from readers.

WARNING
Some of the stunts and activities in this book are
undertaken by experts and should not be attempted by
anyone without adequate training and supervision.

CONTENTS

PAGE 27

INTRODUCTION
4

HIGH AND MIGHTY
6
monster trucks

FAST TRACKERS
8
magnificent motorbikes

PEDAL POWER
on your bike!
10

MAGNIFICENT MOTORS
12
cool cars

WACKY RACERS
14
out of the ordinary

PRIVATE TRANSPORTERS 16
just for one

NEED A LIFT? 18
heavy haulers

HOME MADE 20
art cars and bikes

MUSCLED UP 22
human-powered machines

CRAZY TRANSPORT 24
far out!

LITTLE AND LARGE 26
extreme vehicles

ROBOTS ARE REAL! 28
man machines

FOR SAIL 30
wind power

WATER BABIES 32
boats and ships

UP, UP AND AWAY 34
balloons

SLOW DOWN! 36
parachutes

FULL SPEED AHEAD 38
jet thrust

IN FULL FLIGHT 40
airliners

IN A SPIN 42
vertical take-off

BLAST OFF 44
rocket power

INDEX 46

PAGE
25

PAGE
11

MEAN MACHINES

on the move

Feeling the need for speed? Wish your dad's car was bigger than anyone else's? Or perhaps robots are more your thing? Humans have invented some mighty machines that let us go faster than ever before, reach other planets, soar through the skies, or simply attract attention from unsuspecting passers-by.

Take a trip around your favourite mechanical and moving things with this fun but factual book. Learn about the science of flight, put some wind in your sails, and boost your va-va-voom with special Ripley's fascinating facts and amazing 'Believe It or Not!' stories from around the world. What are you waiting for? Off you go!

In 1974 a Monster Truck called Bigfoot (see page 6) was the first Monster Truck to drive over cars and crush them.

1

Big as they are, Monster Trucks can perform cool stunts such as wheelstands, jumps and doughnuts.

HERE TO HELP...
Of course, this book is full to bursting with fab facts and informative text – but look out for the six key features (numbered here). They will help you find out even more about machines – fun, facts, stories, it's all here!

Ripley explains... **2**

Monster Trucks first became popular in the 1970s. The Monster Truck Racing Association formed in 1988, set down standard rules about safety and construction. These days, Monster Truck shows make millions of dollars.

TWISTS

MOVE IT!

The words in this book go round and round...round and round and round. It's to make you dizzy, it's because this book is full of TWISTS! Move the book or move yourself, it's up to you...

Vehicles in the UK travelled 474 billion km in 2001 – the same as driving to Pluto and back 40 times.

In the last 40 years, more bikes have been produced each year than cars. It's estimated that about 100 million bicycles are made in the world each year.

About 4,000 robots work for the US army. Some of them were used to hunt for Bin Laden's hiding place in Afghanistan.

What's the fastest thing in the world? Possibly – the world! The Earth is travelling in space at roughly 103,000 km/h, faster than nearly anything else on our planet.

In 2005, Robbie Bolger performed the fastest handlebar wheelie. His motorbike was travelling at 169.19 km/h as he popped a wheelie – sitting on his handlebars with his legs dangling over the front of the bike!

Ripley's Believe It or Not! ③

Don't believe it? Well, you should – this book is full of amazing-but-true stories. Like this unusual vehicle, which is part-Reliant Robin and part-speedboat. It was customised by Englishman John Brown and he gained a licence to drive it on the roads as well as launch it whenever he liked!

TWIST it!

④

A bicycle made for two seems reasonable – but this motorbike is transporting all 34 members of India's Army Services Corps Tornadoes!

Recipe time!

How to make A MIGHTY MACHINE

What does it take to make a Mighty Machine? See what you have in your store cupboards and get inventing. Don't use all of these ingredients unless you're planning to enter the Wacky Races!

- **Engine** (optional) – the bigger the better for increased drive
  Wheels – with sturdy rubber tyres for extra grip
  Fuel – to give your engine super power
  Driver's cab – you'll need somewhere to sit

- If your Mighty Machine is designed to fly through the air, you'll have to add:
  Wings – to get you off the ground
  Tail – for controlled flight

- If it has to fly in space, you'll need:
  Rocket motor – to blast off from Earth

- Or if it's a boat, make sure you have:
  Hull – to keep you afloat
  Sails (optional) – to catch the wind
  Propeller – to speed through the waves
  Rudder – for steering

BIG WORD ALERT!

What does that word mean? Here's where you find out. For example, automotive is anything to do with cars, trucks and other motorised vehicles.

Futuristic fun

A cyborg is part machine and part human – it's short for 'cybernetic organism'. The name was made up in 1960 and applied to space research, but in this century the reality of artificial limbs, pacemakers and implants means that people really can become 'bionic'.

FASCINATING FACT

⑥

HIGH AND MIGHTY

monster trucks

A harness holds the driver safely in the driving seat.

Bigfoot 5 stands nearly 5 m high.

They're massive and mean. They leap in the air and flatten cars. No, they're not flying elephants, they're Monster Trucks. These mechanical giants are the stars of stunt-driving shows that never fail to wow the crowds. A roaring 2,000-horsepower engine gives them a top speed of 160 km/h.

In the hands of an expert driver, they can spin on the spot, rear up on their back wheels and jump nearly 8 m off the ground. But don't get in their way. They weigh more than 4 tonnes and they can crush a car so that it's as flat as a pancake.

It is powered by a monster 7.5-litre engine.

MEET BIGFOOT 5

Bigfoot 5's giant tyres were originally made for the US Army for use on an Arctic snow train. The tyres ended up in a junkyard where builder Bob Chandler found them and transformed them into Bigfoot 5's weapons of destruction. At 3 m high, the tyres are the largest on any truck. Monster Trucks get to crush about 3,000 junkyard cars in shows every year.

twist!

The body is from a 1996 pick-up truck.

Each of the wheels weighs more than a tonne.

it's home!

Sheikh Hamad Bin Hamdan Al Nahyan, from the United Arab Emirates, is a collector of awesome automobiles, including this towering power wagon, the biggest in the world, complete with air-conditioned bedrooms, lounge, bathroom, kitchen, and patio area in the back.

FAST TRACKERS

magnificent motorbikes

Millions of bikers can't be wrong. Two wheels and an engine mean lots of fun. Motorbikes have been around for more than 120 years and they're still as popular as ever. There are motorbikes for riding to work, motorbikes for dirt tracks, motorbikes for looking cool and motorbikes for racing. They're all different.

The strangest are the motorbikes that are specially made for setting speed records. They look like two-wheeled rockets. On 26 September 2008, Rocky Robinson rode one of these crazy machines, called Ack Attack, at a speed of 580.833 km/h. That's nearly twice as fast as a Formula 1 racing car.

A BARGAIN, ONLY £375,000!

Dead cool

Gordon Fitch has created a fitting last ride for keen bikers in Britain. They can have their coffins drawn by a Harley Davidson motorbike.

8.3 litre engine is also used in supercars.

power machine!

The Dodge Tomahawk has a huge 8.3-litre engine from a Dodge Viper supercar – that's four or five times bigger than most car engines. The designers think it has a top speed of about 480 km/h, but no one has ever been brave enough to try riding it that fast. Only ten Tomahawks have been built and, if you want one, it will cost about £375,000. Even then you won't be able to ride it on public roads.

Engine air intake.

Double wheels front and back spread the massive weight.

Special rim brakes.

CUTTING EDGE

Why stop at one engine? This motorbike is powered by no less than 24 chainsaw engines. It's nearly 4 m long and can reach a top speed of 255 km/h.

SOMETHING'S MISSING

Ben Gulak in Toronto, Canada, sits atop his fast-track invention – Uno, the world's first one-wheeled motorbike. To give the ride more stability, Ben put the wheels side-by-side just 2 cm apart and directly under the rider, who accelerates by leaning forward. When the rider leans into a turn, the inside wheel lifts and the outside wheel lowers, so both stay firmly on the ground. What's even more unusual about the bike is that it's all-electric, emitting no fumes.

twist it!

BIKER BEDLAM

In 2004, Indian magician O.P. Sharma rode a motorbike down a busy street in the city of Patna with a black bag over his head. Don't try this at home!

German tightrope artist Johann Traber rode a motorcycle on a high-wire 160 m above the Rhine River in 2003. His father, also called Johann, sat on a trapeze hanging below the bike during the 579-m crossing.

Gregory Frazier of Fort Smith, Montana, has ridden around the world on a motorcycle five times. He's covered over 1.6 million km.

In 2004, U.S. motorcycle stuntman Robbie Knievel (son of the famous daredevil Evel Knievel) made a spectacular 55-m jump over two helicopters and five aeroplanes parked on the deck of the Intrepid Museum, an aircraft-carrier-turned-museum in Manhattan, New York.

PEDAL POWER
on your bike!

Chris Hoy is surely the most successful sprint cyclist of all time. By the age of 32, he had accumulated the following titles (among others):
- Four times Olympic Champion
- Olympic Silver
- Olympic Team Sprint Record
- World Record 500 m
- European Champion
- Nine times World Champion
- 27 times World Cup Gold

Bicycles aren't very big or fast, but they are mighty machines. A bike's diamond-shaped frame is so strong that it can carry more than ten times its own weight. It has no engine, but can keep going for thousands of kilometres – as long as you keep pushing the pedals.

It's sometimes hard enough to ride a bike with two wheels without falling over, but could you balance on just one wheel? Some people actually enjoy riding a one-wheeled machine called a unicycle. You need a really good sense of balance.

Built for speed

The best track bikes are built for speed. Their weight is cut down as much as possible, because heavier bikes are harder to get moving. Anything that might stick out, catch the air and slow the bike down is smoothed out. The bike's body is made in one piece.

The seat is set high to get maximum power from the legs.

The bars are low to make the rider bend forwards into the right position for good aerodynamics.

Four or five broad spokes stir up less air than thin wire spokes.

Skinny, low-drag tyres.

There are no brakes – they are not needed!

The back wheel is solid, because it slips through the air easily.

10

PEDAL MEDALS

In 2005, Sam Wakeling rode his unicycle the length of Britain, a distance of 1,406 km.

In May 2007, Quinn Baumberger set out on a nine-month bike journey the length of the Americas, from Alaska to Argentina. He covered 30,600 km and had 50 flat tyres on the way.

The first two-wheeler was built by Baron Karl von Drais in Germany in 1817. It was called a 'draisine' after the Baron. There were no pedals. The rider sat astride it and pushed it along with his feet.

In the 1860s, bikes were called boneshakers because their wooden or metal wheels rattled and bumped over rough cobbled streets.

A dozen cyclists rode 900 km across New Zealand's South Island in 15 days on unicycles.

Frenchman Hughes Richard climbed the 747 steps of the Eiffel Tower on a bicycle in just 19 minutes in April 2002.

Christian Adam of Germany can ride a bicycle backwards while playing a violin.

...twist it!

It's hard enough to ride a bike in the usual way, but Dutchman Pieter de Hart can ride a bike while sitting on the handlebars and also facing backwards! In 2002, he cycled 27 km like this.

Wheely fast!

In 2008, Mark Beaumont became the fastest man to ride around the world, taking just 195 days to pedal 29,446 km and smashing the previous attempt by 81 days.

THINK SMALL!

Bobby Hunt rides this tiny bike in his stage act. It measures only 7.6 cm from the middle of the front wheel to the middle of the back wheel, and it's only 20 cm tall.

MAGNIFICENT MOTORS

cool cars

It's hard to imagine our world without cars. There are about 700 million of them worldwide – so it's no wonder the roads get jammed sometimes. A few of these millions of cars are special. They are designed to be very fast, or very small, or just very silly.

Cars have been made in all sorts of surprising shapes and sizes. If you fancy driving a car in the shape of an armchair or a hamburger, the chances are that someone, somewhere, has made a car to make your wish come true.

Ripley explains...

Piston   Cylinder

Suck
intake stroke

Squeeze
compression stroke

Bang
power stroke

Blow
exhaust stroke

A car engine works by burning fuel. It happens in four steps, called strokes. First, fuel and air are sucked into a cylinder (suck). Then, the mixture is squashed by a piston (squeeze). The fuel burns and the hot gases push the piston down inside the cylinder (bang). Finally, the hot gases are pushed out (blow). Then it all happens again – thousands of times every second. This 'four-stroke cycle' is sometimes called 'suck, squeeze, bang, blow'.

Awesome

The **Bugatti Veyron** is one of the fastest cars in the world. It has a top speed of more than 400 km/h. That's faster than a racing car or an express train.

transformers!

Brazilian Olísio da Silva and his two sons, Marco and Marcus, have created a real-life transformer. Their Kia Besta van takes just six minutes to morph into a 3.65-m-high robot, accompanied by thumping music, smoke and flashing lights. It took them nine months and £84,000 to create the 'SuperRoboCar'.

The Bugatti Veyron is one of the world's most expensive cars. Each one costs about a million pounds.

The Veyron's engine is in the middle of the car, behind the driver.

The amazing engine is over six times more powerful than a family car engine.

Two pipes on the roof, called snorkels, lead air down into the engine.

When the car reaches a speed of 220 km/h, a wing-like spoiler unfolds from the back.

This couch is no slouch! It can reach a speed of 140 km/h, being powered by a 1.3-litre engine. It is steered with a pizza pan!

DIVER DRIVER

Frank Rinderknecht loves to go for a drive... in the sea! His submersible car, called 'sQuba', can drive on land or underwater. The car flies through the water at a depth of 10 m, whilst the driver and passenger breathe compressed air. Instead of a four-stroke combustion engine, the car is powered by electric motors.

THE CAR'S THE STAR

The first motor race, from Paris to Rouen in 1894, was won by Count de Dion with an average speed of about 19 km/h. An athlete can run faster than this!

Edd China invented the 'office car', an office desk and chair that can be driven like a car. In 2003, it set out from London, England, on a 1,500-km charity road-trip to the south of France.

Kenneth L. Moorhouse designed and built a working car only 1.3 m long and 86 cm wide, with a top speed of more than 200 km/h.

A single day's consumption of electricity in the USA is enough to power a car more than 36,000 times around the world.

twist it!

WACKY RACERS

out of the ordinary

Motor racing is amazingly popular. In the USA, seven million fans watch each NASCAR race. Every Formula 1 race has 55 million people glued to their television screens all over the world.

But 'ordinary' motor racing just isn't enough for some people. They can't look at a lawnmower or a snowmobile without wondering how fast it can go. It isn't long before they're racing each other. You name it, and someone has raced it. Almost anything can have an engine and wheels bolted on for a race. Beds, barrels and even toilets have been turned into wacky racing machines.

A large upper surface captures the sunlight.

The low frontal area reduces energy-sapping drag.

Solar cells change sunlight into electricity to run the electric motors that power the cars.

Solar panels provide power for all sorts of machines, from calculators to the International Space Station. When light strikes a solar panel, it provides the energy to make an electric current flow. The solar panel works like a battery for as long as light falls on it.

BEETLE DRIVE

Odd-looking electric racing cars powered by sunlight take part in the World Solar Challenge – a 3,000-km race across Australia from Darwin to Adelaide.

RACING AROUND

The National Lawnmower Racing Championships in Mendota, Illinois, started as an April Fool's joke in 1992, but proved so popular that it became an annual event.

The annual Furniture Race in Whitefish, Montana, involves competitors attaching skis to various items of furniture and racing them down the nearby Big Mountain.

Every year, bed-racing enthusiasts flock to Arizona for the annual Oatman Bed Race. The teams push their beds down the main street, make the beds and then race back to the finish line to the sound of the Chamber Pot Band.

Here's a tale. Emma Crawford was buried on top of Red Mountain, Colorado, in 1891, but her coffin slid down the Canyon in 1929 after heavy rains. Now, as a bizarre form of action replay, every year in nearby Manitou Springs, teams build and race coffins with a living female occupant.

twist it!

>> chair-raising! >>

Sixty-four participants took part in the Office Chair World Championships, which took place in Olten, Switzerland. Racers sped downhill over 200 m, hurtling over ramps and jumps.

These daredevil racers reach 20 km/h on their motorised beer barrels in Windsor, England.

BIG WORD ALERT!

NASCAR
A type of motor racing in the USA.

FORMULA 1
A motor-racing championship in single-seat racing cars. Races take place all over the world.

Joel King's jet-powered street luge board can reach 180 km/h. The board has no brakes – he stops by putting his feet down. Ouch!

PRIVATE TRANSPORTERS

just for one

Wu Yulu's robot has eyes made of ping pong balls.

It can walk at 2 km/h for up to six hours.

The robot can talk as well as walk.

Wu Yulu spent a year building the robot, one of 25 robots he has made.

If you don't have a bike, there are lots of other personal transporters that you could use instead. You could hop on a hovercraft that is able to fly, or a tiny plane just big enough for one.

In the coldest parts of the world, with thick snow on the ground, a snowmobile is the best way to get around. There are 3 million snowmobiles worldwide, and some of them can scoot across the snow at more than 100 km/h.

Wouldn't it be great to get into a car that in a traffic jam can take off and zoom away in the sky? People have been building flying cars since the 1930s, but you can't buy one – yet.

Sit back and let a robot do the work! This rickshaw is pulled by a robot built by Wu Yulu, a farmer from Mawa Village, near Beijing, in China. Inventor Wu started to build robots in 1986, made from wire, metal, screws and nails found on rubbish sites. Wu was inspired simply by watching people going past his farm, and by thinking about the mechanics of walking.

Larry Neal has come up with a solution to being stuck in traffic. Riding his Super Sky Cycle, you can simply unfold the rotors and take off, leaving the traffic behind you. This personal transporter can take off on a 30-m strip of road, fly at motorway speeds, land, and then be driven home as a motorcycle, before being parked in a garage.

This electric engine could change aviation forever. With a battery pack that lets a small, one-person plane fly for about an hour at speeds of up to 210 km/h, it could be a giant step towards eco-friendly flying.

twist it!

Traffic buster

N203FD

Super Sky Cycle

GETTING ABOUT

In 1949, Molt Taylor from Portland, Oregon, invented the Aerocar, a flying four-wheel car with a removable tail and wings, powered by an aircraft engine.

In 2006, English photographer Roz Gordon travelled the length of Britain, from John O'Groats to Land's End, using 73 different types of transport, including a pogo stick, camel, dog sled, golf cart and stilts.

In June, 2006, South African Adriaan Marais and Marinus Du Plessis travelled 21,000 km by jet ski from Anchorage, Alaska, to Miami, Florida, down the West Coast of the USA and through the Panama Canal.

In 1992, US brothers Andre, Carl and Denis Boucher, along with John Outzen, crossed the snow and ice of the North American polar cap, from the Pacific to the Atlantic, on snowmobiles. The 16,500-km journey took 56 days.

uplifting!

Is it a plane or is it a boat? Neither. It's the invention of Rudy Heeman, from Nelson Haven, New Zealand, who has built a hovercraft that, because of its peculiar aerodynamics, is able to fly.

Millions of tonnes of goods and materials are moved around by trucks every year. But you won't see the biggest trucks of all rumbling past your house, because they're far too big for ordinary roads.

Some carry rock out of mines. These massive trucks are the size of a house. They can carry more than 300 tonnes of rock in one load. Even when they are standing empty, they weigh as much as 190 cars. The massive engine that moves such a heavy machine is as big as 45 car engines and its fuel tank holds enough fuel to fill 20 baths.

Each dump truck can cost $2.5 million.

They work in coal, copper, iron and gold mines all over the world.

The driver climbs a flight of steps to reach the cab.

Fully loaded, a dump truck can weigh 592 tonnes.

Mining dump trucks load up with earth weighing as much as 300 cars.

Each tyre stands around 4 m high.

In 2004, in Whitehorse, Yukon Territory, a dog managed to put a truck in gear and coast downhill while his owner watched television. A passer-by alerted the police after seeing the truck go by with a dog at the wheel.

TRAVELLING LIGHT

The 2,000-tonne space shuttle has its own transporter to move it to the launch pad.

The crawler weighs 2,400 tonnes and each side can be raised and lowered independently to keep the shuttle level as it moves up to the launch pad. The crawler travels the 5.6 km from the shuttle depot at a maximum speed of just 1.6 km/h, burning 353 litres of fuel every kilometre. The journey takes an average of about five hours.

Don Underwood of Louisville, Kentucky, owns a 1954 fire truck with a built-in swimming pool!

twist it!

KEEP ON TRUCKIN'

A locksmith from North Platte, Nebraska, made a truck key by looking at an X-ray of the driver, who had swallowed the key. The new key worked first time.

British sculptor Douglas White created a 4.8-m palm tree from blown-out truck tyres in the middle of a rainforest in Belize.

At the 2006 Kentucky Art Car Weekend, Lewis Meyer decorated the front of his Nissan truck with a sea monster made from bottle tops.

In May 2006, thieves in Germany stole an entire roller coaster weighing more than 20 tonnes from the back of a parked truck.

A major road in California had to be closed in 2006 after a truck overturned and spilled 10 tonnes of cat litter on the road. It took four hours to clean up.

MOVING HOUSE

Ripley's Believe It or Not!

This house in Palm Beach, Florida, was donated to a charity and moved to its new location by truck and barge. The owners built a new house on the vacant plot of land.

>> HUMAN HAULER >>

Krishna Gopal Shrivestava pulled a 270-tonne boat a distance of 15 m in Calcutta harbour using ropes attached to his teeth.

19

HOME MADE

art cars and bikes

Some people have to be different. For them, the same car as everyone else just won't do. One popular way to make a car look different is to give it a special paint job. Painted flames, eagle wings or lightning flashes can turn an ordinary vehicle into an amazing work of art.

Another common way to add a personal touch is to cover a car with... well, whatever you like. Owners have customised their cars and, for that matter, motorbikes, by coating them with everything from postage stamps and coins to fur and cartoon characters.

Complete with lettuce, salad and cheese, Harry Sperl's Hamburger Harley Davidson drives around Daytona Beach, Florida. The bike is just one of thousands of hamburger-related items that Harry has in his home – including a giant hamburger waterbed and a hamburger phone. Each one really is something to relish!

LADLED WITH LOVE

Chuck Weedman from Beaver Dam, Kentucky, customised his motorbike by welding on 1,800 ruby red spoons – giving it a lizard-skin appearance.

mint condition

Ken Burkitt of Niagara Falls, Ontario, Canada, is obsessed with coins, and has covered several cars with them. Each coin he uses is coated with polyurethane, to stop it discolouring or rusting. This MGB Roadster, which is covered in gold-plated English old pennies, is currently on display at the Ripley's Museum in Mexico. Coins are bent into shape so that they mould to every curve of a car.

IT'S A COVER UP

twist it!

One of the exhibits at a stamp fair in Germany was a Volkswagen Beetle car covered with more than half a million postage stamps.

Gene Pool not only covered a whole bus in growing grass but also made himself a grass suit. He watered both daily.

Artist James Robert Ford spent three years covering a Ford Capri with 4,500 toy cars.

Torsten Baubach from Wales covered his Mini with tiger-print fur.

Janette Hanson of Macclesfield, England, altered her Mini Cooper so that it matched her handbag.

ROCK 'N' ROLL MOTOR

School teacher Rebecca Bass from Houston, Texas, and her students created this rock 'n' roll motor that depicts many world-famous musicians – including Jimi Hendrix, ZZ Top, Madonna and Sir Elton John. They covered the car with sculpted Styrofoam, beads, glass, jewellery and albums.

BIG WORD ALERT!

VEHICLE

A car, bus, truck or other machine for transporting people or cargo.

MUSCLED UP

human-powered machines

A cyclist produces about 200 watts of power by pedalling. This much power could light two or three electric lamps. That's not much, but it's also enough to power a specially designed plane, helicopter, boat or submarine.

Every two years, human-powered submarines race against each other at the International Submarine Races in the USA. In the air, the most famous pedal-powered plane is the Gossamer Albatross. Bryan Allen flew it from England to France, reaching a top speed of 29 km/h.

Amazingly, it's also possible for one strong person to drag a 180-tonne airliner along the ground by muscle power alone.

The wings are made from thin plastic film stretched over a plastic frame.

>> DON'T STOP! >>

Bryan Allen pedalled for nearly three hours to power the Gossamer Albatross plane across the sea between England and France on 12 June 1979. It weighs just 32 kg.

A propeller powers the aircraft through the air.

Pedals turn the propeller.

DEEP THOUGHTS

Students from the University of Quebec, Canada, built a craft that holds the record for the fastest human-powered submarine. Just 4.8 m long, Omer 5 reached 15 km/h in 2007. It has a crew of two. One person turns the propeller by pushing pedals and a second person steers the sub. It's a 'wet' submarine, which means it is full of water. The crew wears diving gear.

Greg Kolodziejzyk has pure pedal power. In 2006, on a racetrack in California, he cycled a mammoth 1,041 km in 24 hours and clocked up the fastest time ever for pedalling 1,000 km – he took just 23 hours 2 minutes. His Critical Power bike is no ordinary two-wheeler. He rides it lying down. It can reach speeds of 100 km/h and has a cruising speed of 50 km/h on a flat road.

FASCINATING FACT!

In 2006, 72-year-old Chinese grandmother Wang Xiaobei pulled a truck loaded with people for 10 m – with her teeth!

In 2005, Zhang Xingquan from China not only pulled a family car using his ear, he did it while walking on raw eggs – without breaking them.

In 2000, 20 men pulled a dump truck around a car park in Kenosha, Wisconsin, for an hour non-stop, covering a distance of 5 km.

In 1909, Walter Flexenberger invented the Sea Cycle, a catamaran powered by pedalling a paddlewheel turned by pedalling a bicycle.

PHEW!

Eleven-year-old Bruce Khlebnikov towed a plane with a rope attached to his hair on 24 May 2001, in Moscow, Russia.

PUSH HEEL IN

PUSH HEEL IN

OMER 5

Gamini Wasnatha Kumara pulled a 40-tonne railway carriage 25 m in Colombo, Sri Lanka, in 2001, by means of a rope gripped between his teeth.

In Beijing a group of people demonstrate how pedal power can generate electricity that can be stored in portable rechargeable batteries. The batteries are then able to power electrical appliances, such as washing machines.

DID YOU KNOW?

The first submarines were human-powered. In 1620, a Dutchman, Cornelis Drebbel, designed a wooden submersible vehicle encased in leather. It was able to carry 12 rowers and a total of 20 men. Amazingly, the vessel could dive to a depth of 5 m and travel 10 km. The crew turned the propeller by hand.

CRAZY TRANSPORT

far out!

If you're bored with travelling in the usual ways, there are some more exciting ways to get around.

Those of you who are really brave could try being fired out of a circus cannon. You could fly 45 m through the air at up to 80 km/h. Or take a leaf out of Felix Baumgartner's book. In 2003, he strapped a 1.8-m wing to his back and jumped out of a plane. He glided 35 km from England to France across the English Channel. You could try fitting rockets to a car, or a jet engine to a boat. Jet-powered racing boats, called hydroplanes, can reach speeds of more than 350 km/h.

>>UP, UP AND AWAY>>

NASA insists that astronauts from the space shuttle or International Space Station wear a SAFER jet pack for spacewalks. If they drift away from the spacecraft, they can use it to fly back to safety. Crazily they fly through space, miles from Earth.

LED

In-suit drink bag.

Oxygen and temperature controls.

The SAFER pack attaches to the bottom of a normal space backpack.

SAFER JET-PACK

SAFER stands for Simplified Aid For EVA Rescue. It works by sending out jets of nitrogen gas. There are 24 jets pointing in three different directions (up and down, backwards and forwards, and side to side). By choosing which jets to use, the astronaut can vary his or her direction.

On March 5, 2005, 47 people went surfing on Australia's Gold Coast on a single massive surfboard measuring 12 m long and 3 m wide.

Tim Arfons gets around on a jet-powered barstool. The stool reached speeds of 64 km/h at a raceway in Norwalk, Ohio.

In 2006, two British women, Antonia Bolingbroke-Kent and Jo Huxster, drove a three-wheel taxi, called a tuk-tuk, 19,000 km from Thailand to England through 12 countries.

David Smith, from Missouri, USA, used a cannon to fire himself across the US/Mexican border. He waved his passport as he flew past customs control.

BIG WORD ALERT!

NASA

The National Aeronautics and Space Administration – the organisation that carries out space exploration for the USA.

Paul Stender's Port-O-Jet consists of a wooden washroom hut powered by a 50-year-old, 340-kg Boeing jet engine. It travels at 74 km/h and throws 10-m fireballs from the burner at the back. He drives it while seated on the original toilet inside.

WAY TO GO!

This bride and her bridesmaids rode to her wedding in a tractor bucket in China in 2008. The groom arrived in his own tractor bucket, also decorated with balloons.

LITTLE AND LARGE

extreme vehicles

Did you know that you can stretch a car and make it longer? Not like a rubber band – a stretch limo is a luxury car made longer by cutting it in two and putting an extra section in the middle. Whereas an ordinary car is 4 or 5 m long, stretch limos are usually about 8.5 m, but the world's longest is 30.5 m long. However, some people think that small is beautiful. The tiniest cars are less than 1 m high, and the most minuscule planes are just 4 m long. That's about the same length as a car.

ROOM FOR EVERYONE

Meet one long, long limo, made by Jay Ohrberg – known as 'The King of Show Cars'. This lengthy motor is 30 m long and has a helicopter landing site at the back. Add some friends... and drive!

Driven mad

Gregory Denham from California, USA poses at the wheel of his Dream Big motorbike. Rumoured to be the biggest motorbike in the world, it stands a whopping 3.35 m high and 6.2 m long. Denham wanted a bike that could perform like a Monster Truck, so he went ahead and built one!

Room for one

The Bede BD-5J is a 4-m-long plane, powered by a tiny jet engine with a top speed of 483 km/h. With room enough for just one, it was piloted by 007 in the James Bond film *Octopussy*.

Let's compare...

The titchy Bede BD-5J with the world's biggest airliner, the Airbus A380

AIRBUS A380

A380

	Height	Length	Max weight	Wingspan	Max speed
Bede BD-5J	1.7 m	3.7 m	385 kg	5.2 m	483 km/h
Airbus A380	24.1 m	73 m	560,000 kg	79.8 m	945 km/h

Check out the bags of lead shot, designed to keep the nose down.

twist it!

For more on the Airbus A380, turn to page 40.

Benji Ming, at the Edinburgh Festival, Scotland, was so enraged at the small audiences he was attracting for his shows that he transferred his performances from the theatre to the confines of a Smart car. He delivered a comic monologue to a packed house – an audience of one in the passenger seat.

Twenty-one Malaysian students crammed themselves into a Mini Cooper in June 2006.

Jasper, a black Doberman-Labrador owned by Sir Benjamin Slade in England, travels everywhere by stretch limo.

EXTREME!

Streeeetch!

There's room to be creative with the interiors in this 12-m-long Hummer, owned by Scott Demaret from Bristol, England.

SMALL IS BEAUTIFUL

Designed to seat one person and a shopping bag, the Peel P50 was a three-wheeled micro-car, first produced in 1963. It had one door, a single windscreen wiper and only one headlight. With vital statistics of just 134 cm by 99 cm, its minuscule frame weighed in at only 59 kg, but could manage a speed of 61 km/h. Handy for slipping into that confined parking space, the Peel had just one drawback – no reverse gear!

ROBOTS ARE REAL!

man machines

The robots are coming! Robots in films are often walking, talking machines that look like metal people. Real robots are often not quite so lifelike, but there are more than six million robots in the world today.

A million of them are industrial robots. These are computer-controlled arms that help to make things in factories. The other five million or so are service robots. These include robot toys, vacuum cleaners and lawnmowers. Honda's ASIMO robot (see far right) is a real walking, talking humanlike robot. ASIMO is 1.3 m tall and weighs 54 kg. It can walk at 2.5 km/h and even run a little faster.

Mighty muncher

6-m-long flames shoot from its nostrils.

Robosaurus is a 12-m-tall robot that can lift, crush, burn and bite. Created by American inventor Doug Malewicki, it's as high as a five-storey building and is controlled by a human pilot strapped inside the monster's head. As flames jet out of its nostrils, its jaws can tear into a car, ripping it in two.

A large truck engine in the tail powers the beast.

Its jaws crush with a force of 9,000 kg – powerful enough to bite a car in two.

The word robot was used for the first time in a theatre play called Rossum's Universal Robots by the Czech writer Karel Capek in 1921.

Robosaurus weighs 26 tonnes.

UNREAL

Japanese engineers have developed a robotic wine taster that can tell the difference between 30 different types of grape.

Two Scottish inventors have made a robotic bird of prey to scare off pigeons. The robot falcon sounds like a real bird and can even call the owner by mobile phone to warn that its battery is running low.

US government scientists have developed a tiny solar-powered robot fly that weighs less than a paperclip. Its inventors believe it could be used for spying.

The Toyota Motor Corporation built a robot that can play the violin. At its launch, the 1.7-m-tall robot violinist played 'Pomp and Circumstance', a piece of well-known music written by Edward Elgar.

twist it!

>> HOW DO YOU DO? >>

This robot wants to be a real boy! The iCub acts like a human toddler, even making lots of noise — but it can be turned off when it just gets too much!

DOUBLE TAKE

Zou Renti, from Xi'an, China, and his twin appeared at a robotics conference in Beijing in October 2006 – except his twin was not flesh and blood but a fully operational robotic 'clone' of himself.

Astro-bot

Honda's ASIMO robot looks like a small astronaut wearing a backpack. It is 1.3 m tall and if you hold out your hand, ASIMO gives you a handshake. It can walk, climb stairs, run, avoid things in its way and recognise faces. It also knows when someone says its name and can answer questions. ASIMO stands for Advanced Step in Innovative MObility. When its battery is running low, the clever robot will walk to a charging station for recharging.

FOR SAIL.

If your boat doesn't have an engine, you could roll up your sleeves and row it, or you could hoist a sail and let the wind do the work.

A small boat is fun to sail, but a big racing yacht is one of the most exciting ways to travel. Racing yachts can slice through the waves at 55 km/h. Super yachts more than 30 m long can go even faster. A few of the 50,000 ships that carry goods and materials around the world have been built with sails too. Using wind power instead of engines saves fuel.

wind power

CLOSE TO THE WIND

The Wind Surf is a cruise liner that can be powered by either computer-controlled sails or engines. Its sails unfurl automatically from the 50-m-tall masts within two minutes of pushing a button on the ship's bridge. Using only sails, its top speed is about 24 km/h, about the same as its maximum speed on engine power.

Each mast is 50 m tall.

The sails are made from a strong synthetic fabric and cover an area of 2,500 sq m.

BIG WORD ALERT!

CAPSIZED
Upturned. A capsized boat is one that has rolled upside-down.

The ship can carry 308 passengers and has seven decks.

The ship is 187 m long, 20 m wide and weighs nearly 15,000 tonnes.

WIND SURF

WATER WAYS

Japanese sailor Kenichi Horie spent three months sailing alone across the Pacific Ocean on a yacht made from beer barrels.

British woman Hilary Lister sailed across the English Channel between England and France in August 2005, even though she could not move her arms or legs. She steered her yacht by sucking and blowing through tubes that operated the rudder and sails.

During a round-the-world voyage in 1997, British yachtsman Tony Bullimore survived for five days underneath his capsized yacht in the icy Southern Ocean until help arrived.

When a Russian yacht lost its rudder in the Southern Ocean in 2005, the crew replaced it with a cabin door.

>> PLAIN SAILING >>

French vet Raphaela Le Gouvello crossed the Indian Ocean on a sailboard just 8 m long and 1.2 m wide. The 6,300-km journey took 60 days. Raphaela spent eight hours a day at the sail. She has also crossed the Atlantic and Pacific Oceans and the Mediterranean Sea by sailboard.

Ripley's Believe It or Not!

BELUGA PROJECTS

powered by SkySails

BRICK BOAT

It took Peter Lange from New Zealand three months to build his 6-m-long brick boat using 676 bricks. Amazingly, it didn't sink!

Even enormous cargo ships can be wind powered. SkySails are huge computer-controlled kites that give extra power and help save fuel.

Ripley explains...

Thrust

Sail

Low pressure

BOAT

Wind direction

High pressure

A yacht sail works like an aircraft wing. When a sail fills with air, it forms the same curved shape as a wing. This changes the flow of air to create low pressure. The low pressure pulls the boat along. It can move a yacht in a different direction from the wind by setting the sails at the correct angle.

31

WATER BABIES

boats and ships

The biggest and heaviest machines that have ever moved across Earth's surface are ships. Large ships are usually made from steel, while smaller boats are made from wood or plastic.

People have tried building boats from different materials. In 1970, the Norwegian Thor Heyerdahl sailed across the Atlantic Ocean in a boat made from bundles of grass-like reeds tied together!

The carrier produces its own electricity – enough for 100,000 people.

The carrier extracts salt from sea water to make its own fresh water – more than 1.5 million litres every day.

PLANE AMAZING!

The US Navy's Nimitz class warships are nuclear-powered floating airports. Each of these ten aircraft carriers is 332 m long, weighs 88,000 tonnes and carries more than 80 aircraft.

One aircraft carrier costs about £3.2 billion.

MILK FLOAT

Inspired by the milk cartons on his breakfast table, Frank Bölter folded some Tetrapack paper – which is what cartons are often made from – and made a 9-m-long boat. He launched it on the River Elbe in Germany in 2007.

UP AND OVER

One minute it's a ship, the next it's a floating platform for scientists at the Scripps Institute of Oceanography in San Diego, California. Most of the 108-m-long FLIP (Floating Instrument Platform) can be flooded with water to make the stern sink and flip the bow into the air.

BY THE WAY...

During World War II, a British scientist came up with the idea of using icebergs as aircraft carriers. Although a model was built on a lake in Canada in 1943, the plan was scrapped because the ice split too easily.

twist it!

A regatta held on the Mohawk River near Canajoharie, New York, involves boats made from recycled materials, including plastic milk cartons and bottles.

In 2003, Robert McDonald from Emmeloord in the Netherlands stayed afloat for 19 minutes in a boat made from 370,000 lollipop sticks.

In March 2003, comedian Tim Fitzhigham rowed a kayak made of paper 257 km down the River Thames. When it leaked during the eight-day journey, he sealed the holes with sticky tape.

James Castrission and Justin Jones rowed their kayak 3,300 km across the Tasman Sea between Australia and New Zealand. Their voyage took 62 days of paddling up to 18 hours a day.

In 1991, archaeologists in Egypt found a fleet of wooden boats, each 18 m long, built nearly 5,000 years ago.

FLOAT YOUR BOAT

UP, UP AND AWAY

balloons

Balloons and airships are actually lighter than air. They contain a gas that weighs less than the air around them. Airships are filled with helium, whereas most balloons are filled with hot air. Hot air is lighter than cold air – that's why smoke floats upwards from a fire.

Airships are powered by engines and propellers, and they can be steered, but balloons drift wherever the wind blows them. Every year, more than 700 balloons take part in the world's biggest balloon festival in Albuquerque, New Mexico.

The first creatures to fly in a hot-air balloon were a rooster, a duck and a sheep in 1783 in France.

MAN POWER

The 46-m-long Action Man that moved through the skies over London claimed to be the world's biggest parachutist balloon.

Ripley explains...

Envelope

Hot air inside balloon

Burners

Basket

Burners above a balloon pilot's head burn propane gas from cylinders in the basket, where the pilot stands. The roaring flame heats the air above it inside the balloon's envelope. The lighter air rises and carries the balloon up with it. The pilot can turn the flame on and off to change the balloon's height above the ground.

BIG BIRD

Balloons can be built in all sorts of shapes, like this eagle. When air is heated by the balloon's gas burners, it expands and fills every part of the eagle.

World flight

In 1999, Bertrand Piccard and Brian Jones flew the part air-, part helium-filled Breitling Orbiter 3 balloon all the way round the world in one non-stop flight – the first time it had ever been done. The balloon took off in Switzerland, and landed in Egypt.

In 2001, stuntmen Julian Saunders, Rob Oliver and Ross Taylor had a cup of tea on top of a hot-air balloon 1,500 m over Melbourne, Australia.

Helium

Hot air

Gondola

The balloon was in the air for 19 days 21 hours 55 minutes and flew a total distance of 46,814 km.

When fully inflated, the balloon stood 55 m tall.

Propane gas fuelled six burners that heated air in the balloon.

The crew travelled inside a sealed capsule, called a gondola, hanging underneath the balloon.

The gondola had flying controls and instruments at one end, a bed in the middle and a toilet at the other end.

Winds blew the balloon along at up to 176 km/h.

Frenchman Henri Giffard built the first airship and flew it 25 km from Paris to Trappe on 24 September 1852.

A LOT OF HOT AIR

At an air base in Chambley, France in 2005, 261 balloons lined up to float into the air at the same time.

Ripley's — Believe It or Not!

105 balloons

COUCH LIFT

4,267 m up!

Kent Couch made a 322-km flight over the state of Oregon, USA, in 2007 while sitting on a lawn chair. The chair was held aloft by 105 balloons filled with helium. Couch reached a height of 4,267 m and controlled his height by dropping water to go higher, or popping balloons to go down. As the wind blew him towards mountains, he popped some balloons and landed in a field near Union, Oregon. The flight lasted 8 hours 45 minutes.

CHAIR LIFT

Balloon pilot Pete Dalby floated over Bristol, England, sitting comfortably in an armchair hanging under a hot-air balloon.

SLOW DOWN!

parachutes

When mighty machines get going, it takes a lot of force to stop them. The fastest vehicles sometimes use parachutes to help them slow down. The space shuttle lands at 350 km/h. That's as fast as a racing car at top speed, but the space shuttle weighs a lot more, about 100 tonnes. To help it slow down, a huge 12-m-wide parachute pops out of its tail. It catches so much air that it acts like a brake. Parachutes ease the speed of falling things, too.

Whoa!

The space shuttle orbiter stops with a little help from air resistance, or drag.

Ripley explains...

Canopy

Cells

Lines

A simple round parachute floats straight down, slowed down by air caught underneath it. Most parachutists now use a ram-air canopy that acts a bit like a paraglider. When a ram-air canopy opens, air rushes into pockets called cells sewn into it. The cells filled with air give the parachute the shape of a wing. Instead of coming straight down, it flies like a glider.

The bigger a parachute is – the larger its surface area – the more drag it creates.

HIGH FLIERS

French kitesurfer Sebastien Garat competes in the finals of the Kiteboarding World Championship in Sotavento, Fuerteventura, Spain. Using a wind-filled kite, competitors use the short time between uplift and landing to perform breathtaking acrobatics.

DOWNFALL

The Chinese Shenzhou manned spacecraft lands under a parachute big enough to park 100 cars on – 1,200 sq m.

On 16 August 1960, Colonel Joseph W. Kittinger Jr jumped from a balloon at a height of 31,150 m. He fell for 4 minutes 36 seconds before opening his parachute, taking 13 minutes 45 seconds in total to reach the ground.

When Shayna West of Joplin, Missouri, made a parachute jump in 2005, her main and reserve chutes both failed. She fell 3,050 m and landed in a car park, breaking her pelvis, five teeth and several bones in her face. She survived, along with the unborn baby she did not know she was carrying.

When a skydiver in Pittsburgh, USA, caught his foot on the way out of an aircraft door, he dangled from the plane for 30 minutes until it could land. He was unhurt.

Don Kellner from Hazleton, Pennsylvania, has made more than 36,000 skydives. His wife Darlene has made 13,000. They were even married in mid-air by a skydiving minister, Rev. Dave Sangley.

TWIST iT!

Don't Let Go!

Skydiver Greg Gasson hangs by just one hand from his parachute strap, high above Eloy, Arizona.

ground control

Safely down, and the parachutes are cut free. The Apollo 11 crew await pickup in their Command Module.

The Apollo 15 Command Module 'Kitty Hawk', with astronauts David R. Scott, Alfred M. Worden and James B. Irwin aboard, nears a safe touchdown in the mid-Pacific Ocean to end their Moon landing mission in 1971. Although causing no harm to the crewmen, one of the three main parachutes failed to function properly.

WHAT A DRAG

The jet-powered cars that set speed records are so fast that they use a braking parachute to slow down until they reach a speed slow enough for the car's wheel brakes to be used.

FULL SPEED AHEAD

jet thrust

A jet engine is a big air blower. It blows out a jet of air like a hairdryer, but it blows a lot faster than any hairdryer you've ever used. Air shoots out of a jet engine more than ten times faster than a hurricane and as hot as a blowtorch, so don't ever stand behind a jet engine!

Four of these engines can push a 500-tonne airliner through the air at 900 km/h. Planes aren't the only machines to be powered by jet engines. People have fitted jet engines to boats, cars and even themselves. Jet thrust can also be supplied using water, steam or certain gases.

The jet engine was invented by Frank Whittle in Britain in 1930.

SOLO FLIGHT

This 300 horsepower jet pack enables the wearer to fly at up to 100 km/h and perform tight turns and swoops, soar 9 m up into the air, or hover on the spot. Shooting out two strong jets of water, which provide the thrust, a jet pack flight can last for up to 2 hours.

Sound of mind?

On 15 October 1997, British pilot Andy Green drove a jet-powered car called Thrust SSC faster than the speed of sound. He reached a speed of 1,228 km/h.

Thrust SSC was as powerful as 1,000 family cars or 145 Formula 1 racing cars. It was powered by two jet engines from a Phantom fighter.

JET PILOT

Swiss pilot Yves Rossy jumps out of a plane and flies through the air with a jet-powered wing strapped to his back. When the engines run out of fuel, he lands by parachute. On 14 May 2008, he made his first official demonstration flight, releasing himself from a plane at 2,438 m above the Swiss Alps and using just his body position to change direction. In the following September, he flew across the English Channel in less than 10 minutes at a speed of up to 300 km/h.

twist it!

Giuseppe Cannela attached a jet engine to the back of his mother-in-law's wheelchair, giving it a top speed of about 100 km/h.

Paul Stender's jet-powered toilet on wheels can reach a speed of 64 km/h. He races it against a jet-powered bar stool.

If you're into speedy shopping, try Englishman Andy Tyler's shopping trolley. It's powered by a jet engine and can whizz along at more than 80 km/h.

CRAZY

The first jet engine was a machine called the Aeolipile. It was made by Hero of Alexandria in Egypt 2,000 years ago. It was a hollow metal ball with two pipes sticking out. When water inside the ball boiled, steam sprayed out of the nozzles and made the ball spin.

The American Lockheed SR-71A Blackbird jet-plane could fly at more than three times the speed of sound. At top speed, it flew a kilometre every second.

ENGINE AT THE BACK

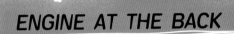

Allan Herridge has attached a Viper jet engine to the back of his Volkswagen Beetle. The car has its original 90-horsepower engine at the front, with the 900-kg thrust jet engine at the back. The jet engine can boost the car's speed from 130 km/h to 225 km/h in less than four seconds.

Ripley explains...

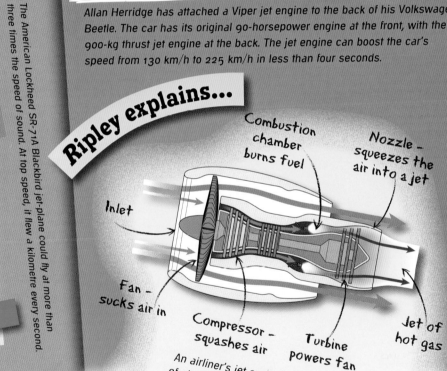

- Combustion chamber burns fuel
- Nozzle – squeezes the air into a jet
- Inlet
- Fan – sucks air in
- Compressor – squashes air
- Turbine powers fan
- Jet of hot gas

An airliner's jet engine works by pushing a jet of air out of the back of the engine to thrust the plane forward. A big fan at the front sucks the air in, and burning fuel heats it. The hot gas flies out of the back of the engine.

IN FULL FLIGHT

airliners

Its giant wings measure 79.8 m from tip to tip. They're big enough to park 70 cars on them.

Sit back and enjoy the view. You're in an airliner cruising through the sky 10 km above the ground. The clouds are laid out below you like a fluffy white field. They hardly seem to be moving, but you're hurtling through the air at 900 km/h, just below the speed of sound. It's sunny outside, but it's also colder than a deep freeze.

The temperature on the other side of your window could be as low as –60°C, and the air is too thin to breathe. Every year, about 12,000 airliners make more than 15 million flights, carrying more than 2 billion passengers.

MIGHTY BEAST!

The Airbus A380 'super-jumbo' is the first airliner to have two passenger decks, one above the other, running the whole length of the aircraft. It made its first flight on 27 April 2005, taking off from Toulouse, France, then spending four hours circling over the Bay of Biscay while engineers carried out tests. It can carry as many as 840 passengers, although most airlines will fit about 525 seats inside it.

FLIGHT OF FANCY

Yes, this really is the inside of a plane. The Airbus A380 is more hotel than aircraft.

Four massive jet engines have to propel a plane that can weigh as much as 560 tonnes.

An African airline bought a Gulfstream jet for US$4.9 million on the Internet auction site eBay.

winglets

Winglets The Airbus A380 has massive wings – its wingspan is the same as the length of a football pitch. If the wings were the same construction as on other airliners, in order to get the massive Airbus off the ground, they would have to be incredibly long: too long for airports, which all have a maximum wingspan of just 80 m. Designers of the Airbus A380 looked to the wings of an eagle for a solution to the problem.

Here's the science The tip of an airliner's wing stirs up the air it is moving through. The spinning air stops the wing from working at its best, so the wing has to be made even longer. Designers noticed how an eagle's wingtips curl upwards as it flies. It gave them an idea. They made turned-up wingtips, called winglets for the A380. Each winglet blocks the spinning air and so the wingspan can be kept to 79.8 m.

If five giraffes stood like a tall tower, each one on the head of the one below, they would be the same height as the new Airbus.

The two decks of the 72.75-m-long aircraft cover a surface area of 500 sq m, the equivalent of ten squash courts.

aner. Quieter. Smarter.

A380

F-WWOW

Fuselage The heavier an aircraft, the more fuel used. The Airbus A380 is longer, wider and has more passengers than any other aircraft, but scientists constructed the outside of the aircraft from an aluminium and fibreglass blend, which is strong yet light.

5,600 people could stand under the shelter of its wings.

More people are killed by donkeys than die in aircraft crashes.

John Davis spent eight years building an exact copy of a Boeing 747 airliner cockpit in his spare bedroom in his modest home. A 1.8-m screen in front of the cockpit shows views of places from the Alps to New York.

IN A SPIN

vertical take-off

Hoverflies are little flies that can stay in the same spot in mid-air as if hanging at the end of an invisible thread. Some aircraft can do the same thing. They can take off straight up into the air and hover in one spot. Most of them are helicopters.

Long thin blades on top of a helicopter whirl around hundreds of times a minute, blowing air down like a big fan. The whirling blades blow hard enough to lift a helicopter weighing several tonnes off the ground. There are about 45,000 helicopters in service all over the world. Helicopters have saved more than 3 million lives since the first helicopter rescue in 1944.

Drive shaft runs through both wings, connecting rotors together, so that if one of the engines breaks down, the other engine will power both propellers.

The tips of the blades whizz round at 730 km/h. The two propellers spin in opposite directions to stop the whole plane from rotating.

A tail fin provides stability.

Refuelling probe. The Osprey uses this to fill its tanks with fuel from a flying tanker-plane.

At speeds of up to 507 km/h, the V-22 Osprey flies twice as fast as a helicopter.

WHAT A CHOPPER! OR IS IT?

The V-22 Osprey takes off like a helicopter. Then its engines and propellers tilt forwards and it flies like a plane. This means it can take off and land almost anywhere, even in remote parts of the world where there is no runway. Built for the military and perfect for use on aircraft carriers, each V-22 Osprey costs about £65 million.

The Osprey can carry 24 passengers.

The Russian Mil Mi-26 is a giant among helicopters. It can carry more than 80 people or 20 tonnes of cargo.

MASTER STROKE

Leonardo da Vinci (1452–1519) made a sketch of a flying machine that seems to anticipate the helicopter, though it's not clear how he thought it would work.

uplifting!

Helicopters usually land with ease, but this one had strongman Franz Muellner to contend with. When the 1,800-kg aircraft landed on his shoulders, he managed to hold it off the ground for nearly a minute in Vienna in 2006.

SPIN IT!

Alexander van de Rostyne created a tiny helicopter called the Pixelito, weighing only 6.9 g.

In 2003, Jonathan Strickland from Inglewood, California, made his first solo flights in a plane and a helicopter on the same day when he was only 14 years of age. He had to go to Canada to do it, because US pilots have to be at least 16 years old.

In 2005, Frenchman Didier Delsalle landed his helicopter on top of the world's highest mountain, Mount Everest, at a height of 8,848 m.

In March 2007, a moose that had been shot with a tranquiliser dart near Gustavus, Alaska, charged the hovering helicopter it had been shot from, and brought it down!

Frenchman Gustave de Ponton d'Amécourt invented the word helicopter in 1861.

SPIN IT!

43

BLAST OFF
rocket power

Three… two… one… lift off. If you want to be an astronaut, you'll need a rocket. It's the only way to get into space and it's the boldest, fastest journey you will ever make. The mighty **Saturn V** rocket launched astronauts on their way to the Moon. Today, rocket power takes astronauts to the International Space Station. By the end of 2008, nearly 500 people from 39 countries had hitched a ride on a rocket into space. Rockets blast satellites into orbit too, and they send probes to the Moon and planets. Back here on Earth, smaller firework rockets light up the sky at special events and celebrations.

Ariane 5 can launch satellites weighing up to 10 tonnes.

Each of the two booster rockets weighs 260 tonnes.

ARIANE 5

Upper stage

Ariane 5 made its first flight in 1996.

eutelsat

ariane space
service & solutions

Payload

An Ariane 5 rocket stands 52 m high and at lift-off weighs 780 tonnes.

Ariane 5 rockets launch satellites for the European Space Agency (ESA). They blast off from ESA's spaceport in French Guiana, South America. Ariane 5 is massive. It stands as tall as a 14-story building and weighs as much as 600 cars. It is actually four rockets linked together. The core stage and two booster rockets fire first. When their fuel is used up, they fall away and the upper stage fires to place the cargo in orbit around Earth.

High point

SpaceShipOne rocketed into history in 2004, when it became the first private, manned spacecraft to reach a height of 100 km. In doing this, its team members won the £6.5 million Ansari X Prize in a competition to encourage civilian spaceflight.

Core stage

Booster rocket

esa

cnes

Ripley explains...

A rocket burns fuel to produce a jet of hot gas. Fuel burns only when it mixes with oxygen. There is no oxygen in space, so a rocket has to carry its own oxygen, or a chemical with lots of oxygen in it. It's called the oxidiser. The fuel and oxidiser mix together and burn. The jet of gas they make pushes the rocket through the air into space. Ariane 5 carries 150 tonnes of liquid oxygen.

Fuel

Oxidiser

Pump

Combustion chamber

Jet of hot gas

Nozzle

BIG WORD ALERT!

BOOSTER

A rocket that gives extra power for take-off.

LIFT OFF

In June 1987, lightning triggered the launch systems of three rockets at NASA's Wallop's Island launch site in Virginia, USA. The rockets were fitted with instruments for studying lightning.

When Gene Roddenbury, the creator of Star Trek, died, his ashes were launched into space by a Pegasus rocket, which will circle the Earth for years.

The Beijing Weather Modification Office uses rockets to spread chemicals in clouds so that they rain on farming areas.

A rocket can fly to the Moon faster than a 19th-century stagecoach could travel from one end of England to the other.

The Aerospace Industries Association of America runs a contest for students to build a model rocket that can fly to a height of 259 m while towing two raw eggs, and then parachute the eggs to the ground without breaking them.

On 23 October 1970, Gary Gabelich drove his rocket-powered car, Blue Flame, at 1,001 km/h on the Bonneville Salt Flats in Utah, USA.

The central part of Ariane 5 contains the main engine. On either side are two rockets that provide almost 90% of the thrust at take-off and for the first 130 seconds after launch.

twist it!

INDEX

Bold numbers refer to main entries; numbers in *italic* refer to the illustrations

A

Aeolipile 39
aerodynamics, bicycles 10, *10*
Aerospace Industries Association 45
air
  car engines 12
  jet engines 38
  parachutes 36
Airbus A380 "super-jumbo" **40–41**
aircraft carriers
  icebergs as 33
  Nimitz class 32, *32*
  V-22 Osprey 42, *42*
airplanes
  airliners **40–41**
  cockpit built in bedroom 41, *41*
  crashes 41
  human-powered 22
  jet engines 38, 39, *39*
  one-man planes 17, *17*
  strongmen 22, 23
  V-22 Osprey 42, *42*
  very small 26, 27, *27*
airships 34, 35
Allen, Bryan 22, *22*
Amécourt, Gustave de Ponton d' 43
Apollo missions 37, *37*
Ariane 5 rocket **44–45**
ASIMO robot 28, 29, *29*
astronauts
  jet-powered spacesuits 24, *24*
  parachutes 37, *37*
  rockets 44

B

balloons **34–35**, 37
barstools, jet-powered 25, 39
bed-racing 15
beer barrels
  motorized *15*
  yacht made of 31
bicycles 5, **10–11**, 22, 23, *23*
bird of prey, robotic 29
blades, helicopters 42, *42*
boats
  in ancient Egypt 33
  built of bricks 31, *31*
  capsized 30, 31
  flipping upright 33, *33*
  human-powered 22, 23
  icebergs as aircraft carriers 33
  jet-powered 24, 38
  made of lollipop sticks 33
  made of recycled materials 33
  Nimitz class warships 32, *32*
  paper 33, *33*
  paralysed sailor 31
  pulling with teeth 19, *19*
  reed raft 32
  rudder replaced with cabin door 31
  sailing boats **30–31**
  yacht made of beer barrels 31
boosters, rockets 45
brakes, parachutes as 36
Breitling Orbiter 3 balloon 35, *35*
bricks, boat built of 31, *31*
Bugatti Veyron 12, *12*, 13

burners, hot-air balloons 34, *34*, 35
bus, covered in grass 21

C

cannonballs, human 24, 25, *25*
canopies, ram-air 36
capsized boats 30, 31
cargo ships 30, 31, *31*
cars **12–13**
  customised **20–21**
  flying 16, 17
  jet-powered 24, 38, *38*, 39, *39*, 45
  large number of people in 27
  pulling with ear 23
  racing 13, **14–15**
  solar power 14, *14*
  stopping with parachutes 37, *37*
  stretch limos 26, *26*, 27
  theatre in 27
  very small 26, 27, *27*
catamaran, human-powered 23
chainsaws, motorbike powered by 9
chairs
  lifted by balloons 35, *35*
  motorized 13
  races 15, *15*
coffins
  motorbike hearse 8
  races 15
coins, car covered in 21, *21*
compressors, jet engines 39
couch, motorized 13, *13*
crawler, space shuttle 19, *19*

Critical Power bike 23, *23*
cruise liner, wind-powered 30, *30*
customised vehicles 5, *5*, **20–21**
cyborg 5, *5*
cylinders, car engines 12

D

desk, motorized 13
Dion, Count de 13
Dodge Tomahawk 9, *9*
dog, drives truck 19
drag 36
Drais, Baron Karl von 11
Drebbel, Cornelis 23
dump trucks **18**, 23

E

eagles, wings 41
Egypt, ancient 33, 39
Eiffel Tower, Paris 11
electricity 13
  electric cars 14, *14*
  generated on aircraft carrier 32
  human-powered generation 23
  motorbikes 9
  solar power 14, *14*
Elgar, Edward 29
engines
  airliners *40*
  airships 34
  cars 12, 13
  jet engines **38–39**
  motorbikes 8, 9
  rockets 44, *44*, 45
  trucks 6, 18
European Space Agency 44
extreme vehicles **26–27**

F

factories, robots 28
fans, jet engines 39
fireworks 44
flies, robotic 29
flying
  balloons **34–35**
  cars 16, 17
  helicopters **42–43**
  hovercraft 17, *17*
  jet packs 38, *38*
  jet-powered wings 39, *39*
  motorbikes 17, *17*
  rockets **44–45**
  see also airplanes
Formula 1 racing cars 14, 38
'four-stroke cycle', car engines 12
fuel
  Airbus A380 41
  cars 12
  helicopters 42
  rockets 44, 45
  trucks 7, 18
fur, car covered in 21
furniture, racing on skis 15
fuselage, Airbus A380 41, *41*

G

gases
  balloons and airships 34
  jet engines 38
  rockets 45
Giffard, Henri 35
gliders 24
gondolas, balloons 35
Gossamer Albatross 22, *22*
grass, bus covered in 21
Gulfstream jets 40

H

Harley Davidson 8, 20, *20*
hearse, motorbike 8
helicopters 17, *17*, 22, **42–43**
helium, balloons and airships 34, 35
Hero of Alexandria 39
Heyerdahl, Thor 32
Honda 28, 29, *29*
hot-air balloons **34–35**
hotel, in airliner 40, *40*
house, moved by truck 19, *19*
hovercraft, flying 17, *17*
hoverflies 42
Hoy, Chris 10, *10*
human-powered machines **22–23**
hydroplanes 24

I

icebergs, as aircraft carriers 32
industrial robots 28
International Space Station 24, 44
International Submarine Races 22
Irwin, James B. 37, *37*

J

jet engines **38–39**
  airliners *40*
  barstools 25, 39
  boats 24
  jet packs 38, *38*
  spacesuits 24, *24*
  washroom 25, *25*
jet skis 17
Jones, Brian 35

K

kayaks 33
key, X-ray of swallowed 19
kites
  kiteboarding 36, *36*
  wind-powered ships 31, *31*
'Kitty Hawk' (Apollo 15 Command Module) 37, *37*

L

lawnmowers
  racing 15
  robot 28
Leonardo da Vinci 43, *43*
Lockheed SR-71A Blackbird jet-plane 39
lollipop sticks, boat made of 33
luge board, jet-powered 15, *15*

M

mining dump trucks **18**
Monster Trucks 4, *4*, **6–7**
Moon 44, 45
motor racing 13, **14–15**
motorbikes **8–9**
  customised 5, *5*, **20–21**
  enormous 26, *26*
  flying 17, *17*
  wheelie 5
Mount Everest, helicopter lands on top of 43

N

NASA 24, 25, 45
NASCAR races 14, 15
Nimitz class warships 32, *32*
nozzles, jet engines *39*

O

office chairs
  motorized 13
  races 15, *15*
Osprey V-22 42, *42*
oxygen 45

P

paper, boats made of 33, *33*
parachutes **36–37**, 45
paragliders 36
personal transporters **16–17**
Piccard, Bertrand 35
pistons, car engines 12
planets, space probes 44
propane burners, hot-air balloons 34, *34*, 35
propellers
  airships 34
  human-powered planes 22
  human-powered submarines 22, 23
  V-22 Osprey 42, *42*

R

racing
  cars 13, **14–15**
  human-powered submarines 22
  jet-powered boats 24
  track bikes 10, *10*
railway carriages, pulling with teeth 23, *23*
rain-making rockets 45
ram-air canopies 36
recycled materials, boat made of 33
reed boat 32

rescue services, helicopters 42
rickshaw, pulled by robot 16, *16*
Robosaurus 28, *28*
robots **28–29**
  pulling rickshaw 16, *16*
  transformers 13
  working for US army 5
rockets 24, **44–45**
rocks, mining dump trucks 18, *18*
Roddenbury, Gene 45
roller coaster, stolen 19
rotors, helicopters 42, *42*
rowing, across Tasman Sea 33
rudder, replaced with cabin door 31

S

SAFER jet packs 24, *24*
sailboard, crossing Indian Ocean on 31, *31*
sailing boats **30–31**
satellites 44
Saturn V rocket 44
Scott, David R. 37, *37*
service robots 28
shopping trolley, jet-powered 39
skis, racing furniture on 15
skydiving 37
snowmobiles 16, 17
solar power 14, *14*
spacecraft
  parachutes 36, *36*, 37, *37*
  rockets **44–45**
  space shuttle 19, *19*, 36, *36*
  SpaceShipOne 44, *44*
spacesuits 24, *24*
speed

airliners 40
bicycles 23
cars 12
helicopters 42
hot-air balloons 35
human cannonballs 24
human-powered planes 22
jet engines 38, 39
jet-powered barstool 25, 39
jet-powered boats 24
motorbikes 8, 9
space shuttle landing 36, *36*
stopping with parachutes **36–37**
yachts 30
speedboat 5, *5*
spoons, motorbike covered in 21, *21*
stamps, car covered in 21
steam, jet engines 38
stools, jet-powered 25, 39
stretch limos 26, *26*, 27
strongmen
  helicopter on shoulders 43, *43*
  pulling boat 19, *19*
  pulling car with ear 23
  pulling railway carriage 23, 23
  pulling trucks 23
  towing planes 22, 23
stunt driving
  Monster Trucks **6–7**
  motorbike jumps 9
submarines, human-powered 22, 22–23, 23
submersible car 13
surfboard, enormous 25
surveillance, robotic fly 29
swimming pool, in truck 19

T

Tasman Sea, rowing across 33
taxis 25
theatre, in car 27
Thrust SSC car 38
tightrope, riding motorbike on 9
toilets, jet-powered 25, *25*, 39
Toyota Motor Corporation 29
toys
  car covered in 21
  robots 28
track bikes 10, *10*
transformers 13
trolley, jet-powered 39
trucks
  decorations 19
  dog drives 19
  house moved on 19, *19*
  mining dump trucks **18**
  Monster Trucks **6–7**
  pulling 23
  spills cat litter 19
  swimming pool in 19
  wedding transport 25, *25*
tuk-tuks 25
turbines, jet engines 39, *39*
tyres
  bicycles 10
  mining dump trucks *18*
  Monster Trucks 6, *6*, 7
  palm tree sculpture of 19

U

underwater
  car 13
  human-powered submarines 22, 22–23, 23
unicycles 10, 11

V

V-22 Osprey 42, *42*
vacuum cleaners, robot 28
vehicles 5, 21
violin, played by robot 29

W

washroom, jet-powered 25, *25*
water
  jet engines 38
  making fresh water from seawater 32
weddings
  skydivers 37
  transport to 25, *25*
wheelchair, jet-powered 39
wheels
  bicycles *10*
  Monster Trucks 6, *6*, 7
  motorbikes 5, 9
  one-wheeled motorbike 9, *9*
  unicycles 10, 11
wind power **30–31**, 34
wine tasting, by robot 29
wings
  airliners *40*, 41, *41*
  eagles 41
  gliders 24
  helicopters 42, *42*
  human-powered planes 22
  jet-powered 39, *39*
  ram-air canopies 36
  winglets 41
Worden, Alfred M. 37, *37*

Y

yachts 30–31

ACKNOWLEDGEMENTS

COVER (l) © Kirill Alperovich – istockphoto.com, (r) Reuters/Ali Jareki; **3** (c) Michael J. Gallagher, (r) Bobby Hunt; **4** (c) Sipa Press/Rex Features; **5** (l) Ken McKay/ Rex Features, (c) Reuters/Stringer India, (r) © Kirill Alperovich – istockphoto.com; **6–7** (sp) Photo courtesy of BigFoot 4x4, Inc. © All rights reserved, (bgd) © Eric Gevaert – istockphoto.com; **7** (t/l) Reuters/Ali Jarekji, (c/l) Mike Derer/AP/PA Photos, (r) Andy Wilman/Rex Features; **8** (l) Doug Hall/Rex Features, (r) Rex Features; **9** (t) Rex Features, (b) Glenn Roberts, Motorcycle Mojo Magazine/www.motorcyclemojo.com; **10** (c) Reuters/David Mercado; **11** (l) Sean Dempsey/PA Archive/PA Photos, (c) Tina Norris/Rex Features, (r) Bobby Hunt; **12** (sp) Barcroft Media; **13** (t/l, b/l, c/l) Barcroft Media, (c) Patrick Barth/Rex Features, (r) Rinspeed; **14** (l) Reuters/Ho New, (r) Reuters/Toshiyuki Aizawa; **15** (c) Greg Williams/Rex Features, (b) Joel King/Wrigley's Airwaves ®, (t) Reuters/Sebastian Derungs; **16** Reuters/Reinhard Krause; **17** (t/l) Camera Press, (b/l) Gavin Bernard/Barcroft Media, (t/c, t/r) Barcroft Media, (b/r) BP/Barcroft Media; **18** (b/l, sp) Reuters/ Tim Wimborne; **19** (l) Courtesy NASA, (c) Jennifer Podis/Rex Features, (r) Arko Datta/AFP/Getty Images; **20** (sp) Photo © Harrod Blank; **21** (r) © Duncan Walker -istockphoto.com; **22** (c, t/r) © Bettmann/Corbis; **22–23** (b) Official ISR Photo; **23** (l, t/r) Greg Kolodziejzyk/www.human-power.com, (c/r) Reuters/Anuruddha Lokuhapuarachchi, (b/r) Reuters/Reinhard Krause; **24** (sp/r) Courtesy NASA; **25** (l) Michel Redondo/AP/PA Photos, (c) Michael.J.Gallagher, (r) ChinaFotoPress/ Photocome/PA Photos; **26** (l) Built by Jay Ohrberg/www.jayohrberg.com, (c) Volker Hartmann/AFP/Getty Images; **27** (t/l) Copyright © 2006 by Juan Jimenez – Reprinted with permission, (c) (r) Rex Features; **28** (sp) TSGT Joe Zuccaro/AP/PA Photos, (t/r) © John H. Clark/Corbis; **29** (t/l) WENN/Newscom, (b/l) Reuters/ Jason Lee, (r) Reuters/Toshiyuki Aizawa; **30** Windstar Cruises; **31** (t/l) Richard Bouhet/AFP/Getty Images, (b/l) Copyright SkySails, © Photos by Wally Hirsh, corrugated iron sails by Jeff Thomson; **32** (t/l) Reuters/Christian Charisius, (sp) © UPPA/Photoshot; **33** (sp) Bill Call, Scripps Institution of Oceanography, (b/l, b/r) GoldenStateImages.com © Randy Morse; **34** (l) Reuters/Ian Waldie, (r) Reuters/Denis Balibouse; **35** (l) Reuters/Stringer France, (c) © Fabrice Coffrini/epa/Corbis, (b/r) South West News/Rex Features, (t/r) Pete Erickson/AP/PA Photos; **36** (t) Rex Features, (b/r) © Carlos De Saa/epa/Corbis; **37** (t/l) Joe Jennings/Barcroft Media, (b) Reuters/Dan Chung, (t/c, t/r) Courtesy NASA; **38–39** (b) Michael Sohn/AP/PA Photos; **38** (t/c) Jetlev-flyer.com/Solent News/Rex Features, (r) Fabrice Coffrini/ AFP/Getty Images; **39** (r) Harry How/Allsport/Getty Images; **40–41** (dp) Reuters/Charles Pertwee; **40** (b/l) Camera Press/David Dyson, (b/c, b/r) ©Airbus 2004 Camera Press/ED/RA; **41** (t/r, b/r) David Burner/Rex Features; **42** (l) David Jones/PA Archive/PA Photos, (r) Gerry Bromme/AP/PA Photos; **43** (l) Vladimir Kmet/AFP/ Getty Images, (r) Mary Evans Picture Library; **44–45** (dp) ESA/CNES/Arianespace/Service Optique Video du CSG; **44** (l, r) Reuters/Mike Blake

Key: t = top, b = bottom, c = centre, l = left, r = right, sp = single page, dp = double page, bgd = background

All other photos are from Ripley Entertainment Inc.

All artwork by Dynamo Design

Every attempt has been made to acknowledge correctly and contact copyright holders and we apologise in advance for any unintentional errors or omissions, which will be corrected in future editions.